EXCUSES,

EXCUSES

D0004125

EXCUSES,

A Compendium of Rationalizations, Alibis, Denials, Extenuating Circumstances, and Outright Lies

EXCUSES

Leigh W. Rutledge

A PLUME BOOK

PLUME
Published by the Penguin Group
Penguin Books USA Inc., 375 Hudson Street, New York, New York 10014, U.S.A.
Penguin Books Ltd, 27 Wrights Lane, London W8 5TZ, England
Penguin Books Australia Ltd, Ringwood, Victoria, Australia
Penguin Books Canada Ltd, 10 Alcorn Avenue, Toronto, Ontario, Canada M4V 3B2
Penguin Books (N.Z.) Ltd, 182–190 Wairau Road, Auckland 10, New Zealand

Penguin Books Ltd, Registered Offices: Harmondsworth, Middlesex, England

First published by Plume, an imprint of New American Library, a division of Penguin Books USA Inc.

First printing, October, 1992
1   3   5   7   9   10   8   6   4   2

(P) REGISTERED TRADEMARK—MARCA REGISTRADA

LIBRARY OF CONGRESS CATALOGING IN PUBLICATION DATA:
Excuses, excuses : a compendium of rationalizations, alibis, denials, extenuating
circumstances, and outright lies / [compiled by] Leigh W. Rutledge.
    p.   cm.
ISBN 0-452-26921-0
1. Excuses—Humor.   I. Rutledge, Leigh W.
PN6231.E87E9   1992
081'.0207—dc20   92–53551
                                                                 CIP

Printed in the United States of America

THE DEVIL MADE THEM DO IT

Famous Excuse #1: "Everybody kept their shoes there. The maids . . . everybody."
— Imelda Marcos, on why more than 3,000 pairs of shoes were discovered in her closets at Malacanang Palace

Famous Excuse #10: "Someone else was using the pencil."
— Dorothy Parker, offering an excuse to *New Yorker* editor Harold Ross for spending the afternoon in a bar rather than her office

Famous Excuse #11: "Well, Jim, *The Sound of Music* was on last night."
— President Reagan, explaining to Chief of Staff Jim Baker why he didn't have time to prepare for the economic summit meeting in May 1983

LEIGH W. RUTLEDGE lives in Pueblo, Colorado, where he spends his days finding excuses not to do his chores.

SOMETIMES A GOOD EXCUSE TO GET OFF THE
TELEPHONE IS HARD TO FIND.

INTRODUCTION

*To give a reason for anything is to breed
a doubt in it.*
—William Hazlitt

Bad excuses are worse than none.
—Dr. Thomas Fuller

Pay attention and listen carefully the next time you're at
work, or having lunch with your friends, or talking on the
phone to your parents: We aren't honest with one another
at all. We each use a dozen, maybe fifteen, sometimes even

twenty excuses a day. "I can't." "I won't." "I shouldn't." "I couldn't."

"The alarm didn't go off." "I only said it for her own good." "The car ran out of gas." "I've been sick with the flu." "The cat did it." "The dog *ate* it."

Shouldn't we all know better by now? Didn't someone (obviously much wiser than the rest of us) once say, "Never explain yourself—your friends don't need it, and your enemies won't believe you anyway"? Haven't we all figured it out by now? Obviously not. We feel cornered and defensive, our backs are up against the wall, the truth (we convince ourselves) will only do more harm than good—and we hand out daily excuses, one after the other, as if the *real* truth ("I overslept," "I *meant* to insult her," "I just haven't felt like talking to you recently") would be apocalyptic.

Excuses are all about a failure of nerve: the fear of losing our friends, of attracting disapproval or disbelief, of being misunderstood. And the sire of all excuses is the single, simple, seemingly innocent question, "Why?"

"Why didn't you come over last night?"

"Why didn't you hand in your homework?"

"Why haven't you called?"

"Why did you buy *that*?"

"Why were you speeding?"

"Why are you late?"

"Why don't you want to make love tonight?"

"Why haven't we received a payment from you?"

We hate it when other people put *us* on the spot, but then, almost by instinct, we turn around and demand dozens of explanations from everyone else. No wonder by the time he was in his sixties, Benjamin Disraeli concluded, with understandable weariness, "There is no waste of time in life like that of making explanations."

Each and every excuse included in this book has been heard (or, yes, even used) by the author. Not a single one was intended to be funny when it was first uttered. Most came from nice, normal, otherwise sane individuals who seemed totally oblivious to the suspicious smile of recognition, or even the laugh of outright disbelief, with which their impulsive excuses were greeted.

The "little white lie"—conceived in the darkness of a car as you race to get to a party you're already late for—may seem increasingly credible as you practice it over and over again, just to get it right, in your own mind. But then, once blurted out for all the world to hear, it suddenly sounds facile, improbable, idiotic. "Excuses, excuses," someone replies sardonically. But then there's no need to worry or cringe. The party goes on, life goes on. And most of the people around you, having heard your foolish excuse, have already filed it away in their minds for their own future use . . .

The Five Primary Maxims of Making Excuses

1. The feebleness or banality of an excuse should never be a deterrent to its use.
2. Always put the blame on something that can't defend itself. Children, pets, inanimate objects, and relatives living in foreign countries make perfect scapegoats.
3. Whine convincingly.
4. Certain ailments work better than others as excuses. No doctor or machine in the world can prove that you don't have that headache.
5. Try to remember that Nature allotted each of us only *two* grandmothers to attend funerals for.

POPULAR EXCUSES
FOR
EVERY OCCASION

I lost track of time.

He started it.

I don't remember anything about it.

Well, you never told me I couldn't do that.

◆

I was going to mail it for your birthday but then I couldn't find it and by the time I found it, it was too late and I was embarrassed to send it to you.

◆

We had a flat tire.

The car ran out of gas.

We couldn't find a babysitter.

The baby threw up all over my dress and we had to go home first to change.

It's not my turn.

I didn't have anything to wear.

I have jet lag.

I'm taking care of a sick aunt. . . . No, this is a different one.

I can't.

I couldn't.

I shouldn't.

I mustn't.

I'd really like to, but my gerbils are having babies tonight.

♦

Our cat got stuck in the sycamore tree. . . . Well, we called the fire department, but they don't get cats out of trees anymore, so my husband went up after her and then we had to wait for the professional tree trimmer to come and get *both* of them down, and by that time it was too late to drop by.

♦

I had a toothache.

◆

I couldn't find my dentures.

◆

I swallowed my gold crown this morning, and I have to wait here until it comes out the other end.

I missed the bus.

♦

The alarm didn't go off.

♦

I couldn't find a parking space.

♦

You have to forgive me—I'm not normally like this.

The Devil made me do it.

Pornography made me do it.

Drugs made me do it.

I guess it just runs in the family.

◆

Everybody else does it.

◆

That's not my department.

◆

Our computer's down.

◆

We must have misplaced your original request.

It's on someone else's desk.

♦

The part you ordered hasn't come in yet.

♦

I don't have the authority to approve that.

◆

Don't ask me—I just work here.

◆

I got stuck in traffic.

♦

I ran into an old friend.

♦

I was pulled over by a policeman.

♦

I locked my keys in the car at work, and then this panhandler with a three-legged dog came up, and . . . oh, nevermind. It's just too complicated to explain.

I've been sick with the flu.

I've been depressed over the ozone layer.

I sliced my thumb off in the Cuisinart.

Saturn's in Scorpio this month. I can't cope.

Go to a shrink? Are you kidding? Shrinks are even more screwed up than the people they treat. Why do you think they become shrinks to begin with?

◆

I would've invited you, but I didn't think you'd enjoy yourself.

◆

I lost your telephone number.

◆

I called but your children answered. Didn't they give you the message?

◆

I was anxious about calling you because I thought you'd be angry that I hadn't called you in such a long time.

◆

The dog did it.

The dog ate it.

The cat did it.

The cat ate it.

The housekeeper must've thrown it out.

◆

Well, it's not like I killed someone or anything . . .

◆

It's Friday the thirteenth.

There's a full moon.

My biorhythms must be off.

I'm just too psychic to go to parties anymore. I spend all night having to sort out other people's vibes.

♦

Oh well, you know us Libras—we're never any good at math [sports, cards, sex, business, balancing a checkbook, parallel parking, etc.].

♦

It was God's will.

We gave at the office.

I don't have any checks with me at the moment.

Oh well, you know, most of that money never gets to the people who *really* need it.

I didn't hear you call me.

I was concentrating so hard on exactly what you were saying that I didn't quite hear what you said.

My hearing aid was turned off.

Well, it worked the *last* time I did it. . . .

◆

We got lost.

I couldn't find the house number.

I must have taken the wrong off-ramp in St. Louis.

I won't go anywhere where I have to go through Utah to get there.

I'm allergic to the sun.

I have a bad back.

I'm not mechanically inclined.

The grass actually grows better if you don't mow it *every* week.

I didn't have my glasses on.

My pantyhose sprung a leak.

Your father had to stay home and wash his toupee.

I just can't think without a cigarette in my hands.

My grandmother smoked two packs a day all her life, and she lived to be a hundred and four.

Even my doctor says it's a bad time for me to quit.

Well, I never said I was totally pure. . . .

◆

I must have been in the shower when you called.

◆

Oh, was that you? The phone stopped ringing just as I got to it.

◆

Listen, I have a call on the other line. Can I call you back tomorrow?

◆

Hello, hello? I can't hear you. Hello? I'm afraid we have a terrible connection. Hello?

◆

I never got your message. The cat sprayed on the answering machine a couple of weeks ago, and it hasn't been working right since.

◆

I don't get paid till next Friday.

I must have put the check in the wrong envelope and sent it to someone else by mistake.

I was going to pay you, but then I had open-heart surgery.

You mailed that bill two months ago?! It just arrived here last week with all sorts of weird markings all over it, as if it had been around the world a couple of times. . . .

I couldn't help myself.

◆

I didn't think it would matter just this once.

◆

Oh, they have so much money, they'll never even notice it's missing.

◆

That man over there said it was okay. . . . Well, he was just there a minute ago.

◆

I forgot we went off daylight savings time last weekend.

I didn't realize what day of the week it was.

I keep thinking it's still last year.

My watch must be fast—I mean, slow.

I'm sorry it's taken nearly six months to get back to you, but we've been *real* busy.

◆

I didn't lie. I just embellished the truth a little to make it more interesting.

◆

The car wouldn't start.

I couldn't find a cab.

I can't come in today—I think I have a fever.

My doctor says I have a touch of pneumonia and need to stay in bed all day.

I'm going through my mid-life crisis.

♦

Oh, I'm too old to do anything like that.

My parents programmed me to be a failure.

We've already made other plans.

◆

I have to go to my son's Little League game.

◆

I can't go anywhere tonight—I'm all out of hair mousse.

◆

Our turtle just died, and we have to bury him before the ground freezes.

◆

My parents' private jet crashed tonight in the Alps,
and the entire Swiss army is out looking for them,
so I have to wait by the phone until someone finds
them.

◆

I must have been vacuuming when you rang the bell.

I must have been in the bathtub . . .

I must have been in the backyard . . .

I must have been in the basement doing
laundry. . . .

That damn doorbell—it only works when it feels like it.

It was *his* idea.

◆

I only said it for your own good.

◆

Well, I'm just repeating what somebody else told me.

◆

He certainly never does *that* at home. . . .

She deserved it.

He *needed* to be brought down a peg or two.

You just can't get things done if you worry about
hurting other people's feelings.

Nice guys finish last.

◆

I'm from Toledo. We don't do that kind of thing in Toledo.

◆

I wasn't drunk, I was just a little intoxicated—there's a difference.

◆

I only had eight beers. If you figure I was there between 9 P.M. and 2 A.M., that only averages out to about one beer an hour. . . .

◆

Boy, was I drunk last night.
I don't remember a thing.

◆

It seemed like the right thing to do at the time.

♦

There are larger issues at stake here.

♦

The voters just don't know what's best for them.

♦

I did it for the good of the country.

◆

I was just following orders.

◆

It was a case of mistaken identity.

I needed the money.

I was framed.

Listen, I really don't belong in prison. All I did was write a couple of bad checks. . . .

◆

I didn't think the gun was loaded.

◆

◆

I could've been a movie star [rock-and-roll idol, writer, film director, professional football player, Broadway dancer, etc.], but I didn't want to hassle with all those phonies and back stabbers.

◆

The sun was in my eyes. . . . We were outnumbered. . . . My hands were full. . . . I'm just going through a phase. . . . Well, I can put wool in my dryer at home and it never shrinks like that. . . . An old school chum dropped by unexpectedly. . . . My analyst says I shouldn't. . . . I started reading a new book and just couldn't put it down. . . . I lost one of my contact lenses. . . . Well, you can't save the whole world. . . . I didn't have anyone to go with. . . . I'm not weaving. The *car's* weaving. . . . It just appeared out of nowhere. . . . My eyes were bigger than my stomach. . . . I'm in a rush. . . . I've got to get up early tomorrow. . . . I just can't find the time. . . . I'll do it when I get back. . . .

No, I really loved the sweater, I'm just allergic to that kind of fabric. . . . Now you see what *you* made me do?! . . . The alternative was worse. . . . The microwave blew up. . . . It's too cold for that. . . . It's too hot for that. . . . Invoice? I don't recall an invoice. . . . I just don't think I'm the best person for the job. . . . I couldn't think of anything to get you. . . . I wasn't near a phone. . . . You forgot to remind me. . . . I had to help a friend work on a car. . . . The phone's been out of order. . . . It was too far to drive. . . . I was only in town for a few days. . . . I had to spend the entire vacation with my family. . . . I was afraid of giving you my cold. . . . It was strictly business. . . . I just like to sit at the blackjack table to meet people. . . .

I'm only human.

◆

FAMOUS EXCUSES

Famous Excuse #1

♦

Everybody kept their shoes there. The maids . . .
everybody.

> —IMELDA MARCOS, on why there were
> more than 3,000 pairs of shoes in her
> closets at Malacanang Palace, 1986

Famous Excuse #2

♦

I never said I had no idea about most of the things you said I said I had no idea about.

> —ASSISTANT SECRETARY OF STATE ELLIOTT ABRAMS, making excuses over his involvement in the Iran-Contra scandal, 1987

Famous Excuse #3

♦

I am from Hungary. We are descendants of Genghis Khan and Attila the Hun. We are Hungarian freedom fighters.

—ZSA ZSA GABOR, explaining why she felt compelled to slap Beverly Hills policeman Paul Kramer after he ticketed her for having expired license plates on her Rolls-Royce, 1990

Famous Excuse #4

◆

We needed authorization. As an oil company we can't just go out and start [cleaning up].

> —EXXON CORPORATION OFFICIAL LAWRENCE RAWL, making excuses over why his company delayed trying to clean up or control the Valdez oil spill for two days, 1989

Famous Excuse #5

◆

I didn't like it and I didn't inhale it.

> —PRESIDENTIAL CANDIDATE BILL CLINTON, making excuses after a previous acknowledgment that he "experimented once or twice" with marijuana in college, 1992

Famous Excuse #6

◆

Goodness knows, the trunk is big enough. It's big enough for two.

> —SOUTH AFRICAN FRANK THOMPSON, rationalizing the fact that he forced his black servant to ride around in the trunk of the family car, 1969

Famous Excuses #7

◆

She molested me. She was just too pushy.

> —ROBERT CHAMBERS, JR. (6'4", 220 pounds), making excuses over killing of Jennifer Levin (5'8", 120 pounds), in the so-called Preppie murder case, 1986

Famous Excuse #8

◆

I haven't made my good film yet.

> —FARRAH FAWCETT-MAJORS, after appearing in a string of big-screen box-office bombs, including *Saturn 3* and *Sunburn*, 1984

Famous Excuse #9

◆

A wretched inn-keeper at Nogent to whom I owe 100 francs . . . threatens to sell Reggie's dressing-case, my overcoat, and two suits, if I don't pay him by Saturday. He has been detaining things, and now threatens a sale.

> —OSCAR WILDE, urgently pleading for money from a friend, Robert Ross, in a letter dated November 23, 1898

◆

I am so sorry about my excuse. I had forgotten I had used Nogent before. It shows the utter collapse of my imagination . . .

> —A CHASTENED OSCAR WILDE, apologizing in a letter a few days later, after Ross pointed out that Wilde had used the phoney "inn-keeper at Nogent" story before

Famous Excuse #10

♦

Someone else was using the pencil.

—AUTHOR DOROTHY PARKER, offering an excuse to *New Yorker* editor Harold Ross after he angrily confronted her for spending an afternoon in a neighborhood bar rather than in her office working

Famous Excuse #11

◆

Well, Jim, The Sound of Music *was on last night.*

> —PRESIDENT REAGAN, explaining to Chief of Staff Jim Baker why he hadn't had time to prepare for the Williamsburg economic summit in May 1983

Famous Excuse #12

◆

His sense of direction was always so bad. There was a family joke about his never knowing what turn to take.

—FAMILY FRIEND, making excuses for Senator Edward Kennedy, after Kennedy drove his car off a bridge (drowning passenger Mary Jo Kopechne) at Chappaquiddick Island, 1969

Famous Excuse #13

♦

We just wanted to live life the American way. We wanted to be stars.

> —ROB PILATUS, of the music group Milli Vanilli, making excuses over why he and partner Fab Morvan didn't actually do the singing on their debut album, "Girl You Know It's True," and then later resisted revealing the secret, 1990

Famous Excuse #14

◆

The governments of proper countries are usually on holidays on weekends.

> —SOVIET SPOKESMAN EUGENE POZDNAYA-
> KOV, stretching to explain why his gov-
> ernment delayed reporting the Chernobyl
> nuclear power plant disaster to the rest
> of the world in April 1986

Famous Excuse #15

◆

I was just clumsy, man. . . . The bottle of rum was on the TV table, and somehow I knocked over the bottle and spilled some of the rum. . . . I started to light a cigarette, and the next thing I knew I was on fire. . . . It just blew up! The bottle of rum!

—COMEDIAN RICHARD PRYOR, explaining how he came to be severely burned in an accident at his home in 1980. Several years later, he finally acknowledged he'd actually been freebasing cocaine when the explosion occurred.

Famous Excuse #16

◆

I couldn't. I carry my cigars in my back pockets and I was afraid I'd break them.

>—BASEBALL PLAYER JIMMY DYKES OF THE PHILADELPHIA ATHLETICS, asked why he hadn't slid into second base during a critical play, 1925

Famous Excuse #17

◆

Oh, that was just an accident that happened.

> —PRESIDENT NIXON, offering an explanation for why one of the key Watergate tapes had a mysterious eighteen-minute erasure on it, 1973

Famous Excuse #18

♦

We may be finding in some blacks, when the chokehold is applied, the veins and arteries do not open up as fast as they do in normal people.

> —Los Angeles Police Chief Daryl Gates, trying to rationalize the fact that twelve blacks "inexplicably" died as a result of L.A.P.D. chokeholds between 1975 and 1982

Famous Excuse #19

♦

I would have written sooner but I got a Christmas tree ornament stuck in my pancreas, and it kept winking on and off, and I was too distracted to write letters.

> —Author E. B. White, making excuses to a friend whom he hadn't written in a long time

Famous Excuse #20

◆

I am *big—it's the* pictures *that got small!*

> —FADING SILENT SCREEN SIREN NORMA
> DESMOND (PLAYED BY GLORIA SWAN-
> SON), making excuses over her expired
> movie career, in *Sunset Boulevard*
> (1950)

Famous Excuse #21

♦

Well, they're multipurpose pliers.

> —SPOKESMAN FOR DEFENSE CONTRACTOR PRATT AND WHITNEY, trying to justify the company's policy of charging the Pentagon $999 each for pairs of ordinary pliers, 1990

Famous Excuse #22

◆

I didn't accept it. I received it.

> —REAGAN NATIONAL SECURITY ADVISER
> RICHARD ALLEN, attempting to justify his
> receipt of $1,000 in cash (and a pair of
> expensive watches) from two Japanese
> journalists after he helped arrange a pri-
> vate interview for them with First Lady
> Nancy Reagan in 1981. Allen was later
> forced to resign.

Famous Excuse #23

♦

My supporters were at their daughters' coming-out parties.

> —PRESIDENTIAL CANDIDATE GEORGE BUSH, making excuses for his alarmingly poor showing in the 1988 Iowa caucases (Bush finished third behind Robert Dole and Pat Robertson)

Famous Excuse #24

◆

It's a real downer.

> —THE ALABAMA STATE TEXTBOOK COM-
> MITTEE, trying to explain why they rec-
> ommended that *The Diary of Anne
> Frank* be banned from the state's public
> school libraries, 1983

Famous Excuse #25

♦

*We've got to pause and ask ourselves: How much
clean air do we need?*

> —LEE IACOCCA, making excuses over De-
> troit's resistance to tougher automobile
> emission standards, 1974

Famous Excuse #26

◆

I was simply furnishing a home. I love music . . . and I don't think a $130,000 indoor-outdoor stereo system is extravagant.

> —LEONA HELMSLEY, refuting charges that her lifestyle was excessive, 1990

Famous Excuse #27

◆

Outside of the killings, we have one of the lowest crime rates in the country.

> —WASHINGTON, D.C., MAYOR MARION BARRY, making excuses for the hundreds of shootings, stabbings, and other murders in the nation's capital in 1988

Famous Excuse #28

◆

A man of action can't wear jewelry; he'll get it snagged.

> —GERALDO RIVERA's excuse to his first three wives on why he never wore his wedding ring when he was traveling out of town

Famous Excuse #29

◆

A crocodile swallowed it.

>—NOVELIST JACK REYNOLDS, explaining to his publisher what happened to the long-awaited sequel to Reynolds's popular first novel, *A Woman of Bangkok*. Reynolds, who lived in Southeast Asia, claimed he'd been walking across a bridge with the manuscript in hand when he'd lost his balance and the pages fell into crocodile-infested waters.

Famous Excuse #30

◆

Anyone can make a mistake.

> —SELF-PROCLAIMED ITALIAN "PROPHET"
> ELIO BIANCO, making excuses at 1:58
> P.M. on July 14, 1960, after he erron-
> eously predicted that the world would
> come to an end at 1:45 P.M. that day

Famous Excuse #31

◆

I wasn't calling as somebody in Washington. I was calling as a mother.

> —LYNNE CHENEY, wife of U.S. Defense Secretary Dick Cheney, explaining her decision to call Yellowstone National Park to demand a summer job for her daughter after the daughter's application for a job there was initially rejected, 1989

Famous Excuse #32

◆

It brought me closer to God.

> —FORMER PTL CHURCH SECRETARY JES-
> SICA HAHN, offering a novel excuse for
> her decision to do a ten-page nude lay-
> out in *Playboy* magazine, 1987

Famous Excuse #33

◆

Yeah, I hit her, but I didn't hit her more than the average guy beats his wife.

> —IKE TURNER, explaining his persistent abuse of his former wife, singer Tina Turner, 1985

Famous Excuse #34

◆

It's not like molesting young girls or young boys.
It's not a showstopper.

> —TEXAS CONGRESSMAN CHARLIE WILSON,
> trying to downplay revelations that he
> bounced 81 checks at the House of
> Representatives bank, including one—
> for $6,500—to the IRS, 1992

Famous Excuse #35

◆

I'd love to kiss ya, but I just washed my hair.

> —BETTE DAVIS, offering an immortal excuse in the film *Cabin in the Cotton* (1932)

SPECIALIZED
EXCUSES

10 Common Excuses Given to Policemen

1. My speedometer must be broken.

2. Your radar gun must be broken.

3. There's never been a stop sign *there* before.

4. Well, the light looked green to me.

5. My gas pedal must have gotten stuck.

6. I was just keeping up with traffic.

7. Where I come from, we don't have to make a complete stop.

8. The guy in the red Camaro was going twice as fast as I was.

9. I'm sick and I have to get to a hospital.

10. I didn't know what the speed limit was.

10 Bizarre Excuses Given to Policemen

1. I don't even have a driver's license, so why do I have to obey the traffic laws?

2. It's the car's fault—I can't control it anymore.

3. I'm almost out of gas and I was rushing to get to a gas station before the tank runs dry.

4. This isn't even my car. How was I supposed to know how fast it was going?

5. I sometimes drive this fast just to meet policemen.

6. I'm being chased by UFOs.

7. I was just trying to get these books back before they're overdue at the library.

8. The car runs so well that 70 mph only seems like 40.

9. My wife kept yelling, "Faster, faster—we're going to be late!" Give *her* the ticket.

10. Mel Gibson always drives like that in the movies.

10 Common Excuses
for Not Handing in Homework

1. The dog ate it.

2. I left it in my locker.

3. I thought you just wanted us to read the chapter, not write a report on it.

4. My mother spilled her coffee on it.

5. I thought it was due tomorrow.

6. I didn't understand the material.

7. My sister and I got our homework mixed up, and she has my math assignment and I have her book report.

8. My mother accidentally threw it in the trash.

9. My family had to go to church, and I couldn't get it done.

10. I couldn't find any pencils to write with.

10 Memorable Excuses for Not Handing in Homework

1. I was mugged on my way to school.

2. The finance company was coming to repossess my parents' television, and I wanted to get in one last night of watching TV.

3. My little brother used it to draw dirty pictures all over.

4. My Aunt Gretchen took it back to Germany with her.

5. I did it all in my head.

6. We had a fire at our house last night, and when I tried to run back in to save my homework the fireman stopped me.

7. The furnace broke down and we had to burn my homework to keep warm.

8. My sister got mad at me and flushed it down the toilet.

9. Dan Quayle never did any homework and look where he is today.

10. My father made me play Nintendo last night.

10 Excuses Used by Lovers

1. I've got a headache.

2. I'm not in the mood.

3. My back hurts.

4. The people in the next room might hear us.

5. I *can't*—not here in my mother's house.

6. Listen, it's not like sex is all that important to a marriage anyway.

7. The dog's watching us. I can't *do* it when the dog's watching us.

8. I'm too tense.

9. I have a big game [concert, rough work day, important deal] tomorrow—I have to save my strength.

10. I'm sorry, but *every* time I look at you tonight I keep seeing your brother Waldo—and you know how I feel about *him.*

9 Common Excuses for Not Having a Cat Fixed

1. I want him to experience sex at least once before he dies.

2. It's not natural.

3. How would you like it if someone did that to you?

4. We want our kids to see the miracle of birth.

5. But Snowball hasn't had a chance to pass on his genes yet.

6. We keep her in the house most of the time, so it really doesn't matter.

7. He'll only be half a man.

8. We think she's perfect just the way she is.

9. Well, he's not really our cat. We've just been feeding him for the last couple of years.

10 Familiar Excuses for Over-Eating

1. I've been under a lot of stress.

2. It's the holidays.

3. I can work it off at the gym tomorrow.

4. It doesn't really matter what I eat so long as I drink lots of water with it.

5. I *had* to have a pizza during the football game. What's a football game without a pizza?

6. I didn't want to insult the hostess by not having one of her homemade eclairs.

7. I'm planning to go on a diet next week so this is really just my last big binge.

8. I needed to make room in the freezer and I didn't want all that food to go to waste.

9. It doesn't matter how much I try to cut back on my eating—if I even smell food, I gain weight.

10. Well, someone had to finish the birthday cake before it went stale.

10 Familiar Excuses for Buying Things None of Us Needs

1. I just had to have it.

2. It was the last one, and I was afraid if I didn't get it now, it'd be gone when I went back.

3. The sales clerk said he'd never seen anyone who looked so good in one.

4. It was on sale.

5. It's a collector's item.

6. Well, you can never have too many shoes [jeans, scarves, houseplants, T-shirts, calculators, tools].

7. I felt sorry for the old lady who runs the shop—no one else was even browsing in there.

8. I've always wanted one, ever since I was a kid.

9. I just felt it was time I treated myself to a little something special.

10. Everyone else was buying them.

When in doubt,
tell the truth.

—MARK TWAIN